CRAFT TOPICS

VIKINGS

FACTS • THINGS TO MAKE • ACTIVITIES

RACHEL WRIGHT

FRANKLIN WATTS

LONDON•SYDNEY

This edition 2008

Franklin Watts
338 Euston Road
London, NW1 3BH

Franklin Watts Australia
Level 17/207 Kent Street
Sydney, NSW 2000

© 1992 Franklin Watts

Editor: Hazel Poole
Consultant: Dr Dominic Tweddle
Design: Sally Boothroyd
Photography: Chris Fairclough
Artwork: Ed Dovey
Additional picture research: Juliet Duff

A CIP catalogue record for this book is available from
the British Library.

ISBN: 978 0 7496 7830 2
Dewey number: 948'.02

Printed in Dubai

Franklin Watts is a division of Hachette Children's
Books, an Hachette Livre UK company.

CONTENTS

THE VIKINGS ABROAD

RAIDERS . . .

The "Viking Age" began in the late 700s, when ship-loads of warriors left their homes in Scandinavia to plunder the coasts of western Europe. These sea-borne raiders, known as Vikings, wreaked havoc wherever they went. They ransacked churches and monasteries, stole treasure, seized prisoners as slaves, and slaughtered anyone who stood in their way.

. . . SETTLERS

During the 800s, these swift and savage raids became more frequent. They also became more organized. Instead of just smashing and grabbing, the Vikings started to settle in the lands they attacked. By the mid to late 800s, they had colonised parts of England, Ireland and Scotland.

The Vikings were adventurers. They crossed the unknown Atlantic Ocean to lands which few, if any, Europeans had explored.

In about AD 870, a group of Norwegian Vikings settled in Iceland, and in AD 982, Eirik the Red discovered Greenland. Although the land he sighted was icy and desolate in parts, he named it "Green" in the hope that others would be persuaded to settle there.

Twenty years after Eirik's discovery, his son, Leif, became the first European to land in North America. A small number of Vikings then tried to settle in America, but their plan backfired. After they had been there only a few years, they ran into trouble with some native Americans and were forced to head back home.

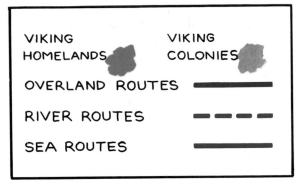

VIKING HOMELANDS

VIKING COLONIES

OVERLAND ROUTES ——————

RIVER ROUTES – – – – –

SEA ROUTES ——————

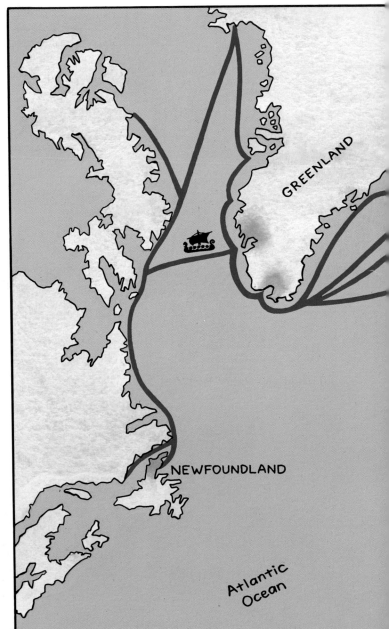

GREENLAND

NEWFOUNDLAND

Atlantic Ocean

... AND TRADERS

Raiding and trading went together, and the Vikings were good at both. They often combined raids with trading expeditions, and sold their stolen goods and prisoners of war at home and abroad.

The Swedish Vikings, in particular, were remarkable traders. They sailed down Russia's main rivers, taking over and setting up trading posts as they went. They even ventured down as far as the Black Sea and Central Asia. In return for slaves and goods from their cold homelands, such as furs, fish, amber, honey and walrus ivory, the Vikings were given silks, spices, silver, wine and glass. These luxury goods were eagerly sought by traders and customers back in Scandinavia.

Viking activity continued in Europe and beyond for nearly 300 years. When it ceased in the late 1000s, the Viking Age came to an end.

▼ *This map shows just how far the Vikings ventured. Although they made their mark wherever they settled, the Vikings were greatly influenced by the people they met.*

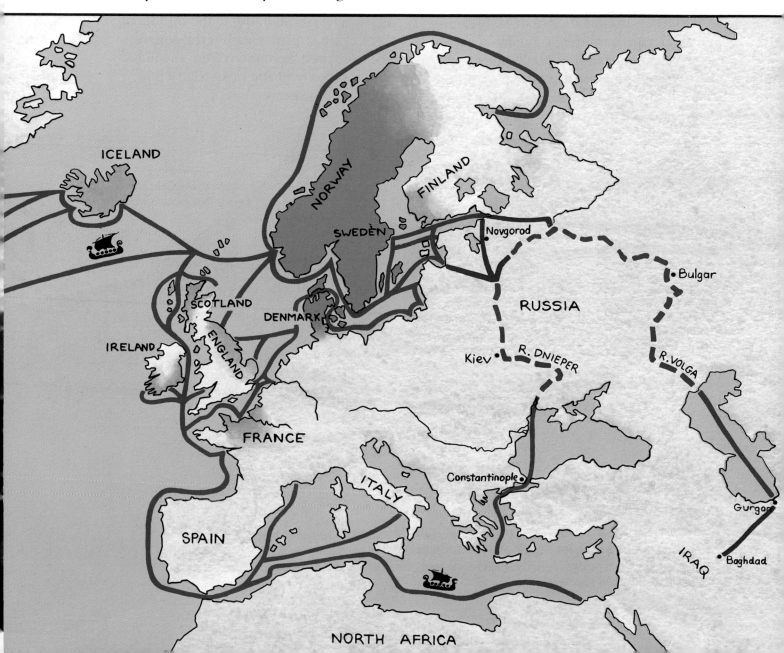

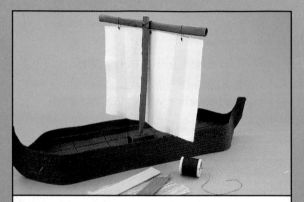

▲ **13.** Glue or tie the two poles together with thread, and slot the mast and sail into place. If your mast wobbles, wedge some plasticine inside its holder.

TO MAKE AN OARSMAN'S CHEST

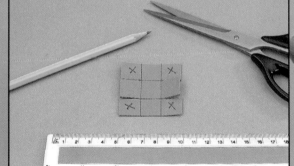

▲ **15.** Mark and cut a square of card 5cm x 5cm, as shown.

Each oarsman sat on a wooden chest, packed with his belongings.

TO MAKE A FIGUREHEAD

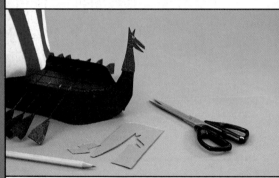

▲ **14.** Trace the shape below onto a folded piece of card. Cut it out, paint it and then glue it to your ship's prow. Now push all the oars into place.

16. Spread some glue on the back of the tabs marked x. Fold them inwards and glue them to their nearest panels, to make a box.

17. Turn the box over, paint it, and glue it next to an oar hole.

When coming into harbour, the Vikings sometimes hung their shields on the side of their ships.

TO MAKE A SHIELD

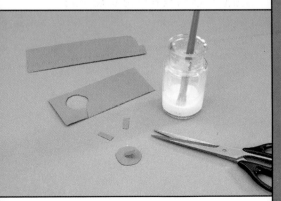

18. Glue a tiny strip of folded card onto the back of a card circle. When you have made as many shields as you need, paint them and hang them along your ship's sides.

LAW AND ORDER

During most of the Viking Age, Sweden, Norway and Denmark each had their own king and royal family. Although each king was the most important person in his own land, he was only slightly more powerful than his nobles.

The nobles, or jarls as they were called, were warrior aristocrats. They owned land, farms, ships and slaves, and financed raiding and trading expeditions.

The crews for these expeditions were mainly made up of free-born peasants, called karls. Karls were the craftsmen, traders and farmers of the Viking world. Some owned or rented farm land. Others worked on a jarl's farm.

The dirtiest and smelliest jobs on any farm were done by slaves called thralls. Thralls had to work hard for their owners, and sleep in a draughty outbuilding. Unlike the jarls and karls, they had few rights in law.

Large Things were like fairs. People set up camp, chatted, traded, and watched their favourite sports.

SORTING THINGS OUT AT THE "THING"

The Vikings didn't have separate law courts and parliaments as we do today. They settled lawsuits and tried criminals at open air meetings called "Things". Each district would hold a Thing whenever necessary, and all the local jarls and karls would be invited to have their say. When everyone had spoken and a decision had been reached, they all clashed their weapons together to show that they were in agreement.

The Vikings didn't have prisons. Most serious criminals found guilty by the Thing were either fined or banished. Banishment was the most dreaded punishment of all. Family ties were very important to the Vikings, and to be exiled from one's family was a fate worse than death.

13

DOWN ON THE FARM

During the Viking Age, most Scandinavians lived in small, isolated farming communities. Crop growing and cattle rearing were their main source of livelihood. However, because much of Scandinavia was covered with forest and mountains, there wasn't a great deal of good farm land to be found.

To make matters worse, the little suitable land available was often hard to farm because of the harsh, cold Scandinavian climate. This land-shortage problem, together with the problems of overpopulation, may explain why so many Vikings left home in search of new lands.

With farm land in short supply, farmers had to be fishermen and hunters, as well. They killed wild animals, such as deer, boars, bears, whales and seals for food, and used animal skins to make tents and sleeping bags for sea journeys. They also used the animals' bones and antlers to make ice skates, spindles, combs and spoons.

Every farmer's life was ruled by the seasons. In the spring, he would plough his fields with an ox or horse-drawn plough, and plant crops, such as rye, oats and barley. He might then spend the summer raiding overseas, before returning home for the harvest.

WOMEN'S WORK

While the men were away at sea, the women were left in charge of the farms. Their tasks were just as gruelling as their husbands'. They had to milk the cows and goats, make butter and cheese, and prepare all the food. In the autumn, when many of their cattle were killed, the women salted the meat to preserve it. They had to make sure that there was enough food to last through the long cold winter months.

The women weren't only responsible for providing food. They also had to spin sheep's wool and beat flax into thread. The flax was then woven on looms into linen, and the wool was woven into woollen cloth. The women used the cloth to make blankets, wall hangings, clothes and ship sails.

Viking children didn't go to school. Instead they had to help with the chores at home, and learn practical skills. The girls were shown how to cook, sew, skin animals and run a household. The boys were taught to plough, hunt, fish and fight.

Not all Vikings lived in farming communities. Many craftsmen found it more profitable to live in trading towns near the sea.

At Home with the Vikings

Viking houses were made from whatever kind of building material was most readily available. Some were built of posts, with a mixture of straw and clay plastered between the posts. Others had plank walls, or turf walls lined with wood. In treeless regions, stone, clay and turf were used instead of wood.

INSIDE A LONG-HOUSE

A jarl and his family often lived in their farm's main building, called the long-house. Long-houses were like gloomy hallways with an open fire in the middle of the floor. They were always smoky because there were few, if any, windows, and only a small hole in the roof to let out the fire's smoke.

Many long-houses were like a living room, dining room, bedroom and kitchen, all rolled into one. They were cramped and uncomfortable, without carpets or sofas to lounge about on. The earthen floors were strewn with reeds, and the benches that lined the walls served as beds at night.

Wealthy Vikings had tables and chairs, but no-one had cupboards. Everyone stored their belongings in wooden chests instead. At mealtimes the Vikings used plates, knives and spoons, but not forks. They drank beer, mead and sometimes wine from wooden cups or glasses. They also drank from cowhorns, which were passed from drinker to drinker.

FEASTS AND FESTIVALS

The high spots of the Viking year were the three major festivals or feasts. The first of these feasts was held after Christmas and animal sacrifices were offered to the gods to ensure good crops in the spring. The second feast was held in April, and sacrifices were offered for victory in the summer raids. The third feast was held after the harvest, to ask the gods for a mild winter.

Feasts were a good excuse to eat a lot and get very, very drunk, so the Vikings held them whenever they had something to celebrate. After the eating had ended, travelling poets and storytellers would thrill everyone with tales of bloody battles and daring deeds. Storytellers, or skalds as they were called, were always made welcome. They wandered from place to place, reciting sagas and passing on the latest news.

Most houses had roofs made out of reeds, turf or wooden shingles.

The benches that lined the walls of a longhouse were sometimes made of mounds of earth.

RELIGION AND RITUALS

Until they became Christians, the Vikings worshipped many different gods.

Their most powerful god was Odin, the god of war. Ferocious and terrifying, Odin thirsted for knowledge. Every day his two ravens, Huginn (Thought) and Muninn (Memory), would fly around the world and report back to him.

Odin was also the god of poets and dead warriors. Vikings who died bravely in battle were expected to go to Odin's heaven, called Valhalla. There they would be free to fight all day and feast all night.

Thor was the favourite god of the karls. They called upon him whenever they were in trouble. They also wore his symbol – the mighty hammer – around their necks, to keep away evil spirits.

Thor was the god of thunder, lightning, wind and rain. The Vikings believed that whenever he raced across the clouds in his goat-drawn chariot, thunder crashed and lightning cracked.

Frey was the god of nature. Sacrifices were made to him to ensure that the crops grew, the sun shone and all was peaceful. His sister, Freyja, was the goddess of love and dead women. Slain warriors who didn't go to Odin's Valhalla joined the dead women in Freyja's fortress.

BURYING THE DEAD

If the spirits of dead warriors and women joined the gods, where did everyone else go after they died? The Vikings didn't have one clear idea about what happened after death. This may explain why they had so many different burial customs. Sometimes they burned their dead. At other times they put the corpse in a large wooden chamber, and either buried it beneath a field or covered it with a mound of earth.

Wealthy warriors were often laid out in ships, which were then buried. Occasionally these burial ships were set alight and pushed out to sea. If an expensive boat couldn't be spared, the corpse was buried in the ground and surrounded by stones arranged in the shape of a boat. Needless to say, poor people were not buried with such ceremony. They were usually just put into a hole in the ground.

The Vikings often buried their loved ones with their most valuable and useful belongings. Perhaps they thought that the dead person would need these earthly possessions in the next world.

Getting started

This book will show you all kinds of wonderful painting projects. Here are some of the things you will need to get started.

Top tip
Collect old jam jars to hold water to wash your brushes in.

Basic equipment
- Paper and card
- Poster, **acrylic** and **watercolour paints**
- Pencils and paintbrushes
- Safety scissors
- **PVA** glue

You will also need some extra items, which are listed separately for each project.

Use a soft pencil (marked 'B' on the side) to sketch outlines before you paint

Use a thin brush for details and a thick brush to paint large areas

Paper
Smooth **cartridge paper** is best for most paints. You can also buy special watercolour paper that does not wrinkle when wet.

Brushes
Brushes come in all shapes and sizes and can be used for different effects. Soft brushes are good to use with watercolour paints. Brushes with stiff **bristles** are better with acrylics.

Take care!

Some projects involve cutting. Always ask an adult for help where you see this sign. ⚠️

Acrylic paints

Poster paints

Watercolour paints

Paints

Poster paints are good for big, bold paintings. Use them straight from the pot or mix with water to make them thinner.

Acrylic paints are thick, bright and easy to mix. Use them straight from the tube or mix with water.

Watercolour paints come in tubes or blocks. They are good for landscapes.

Mix your paints on a special **palette** or use an old white saucer or the lid of a plastic tub or carton.

Top tip

Always carry a **sketchbook** for quick on-the-spot drawings. You can turn them into finished paintings later.

Splitter splatter!

Make a lively painting by spattering paint onto paper with a brush or toothbrush.

You will need:
An old toothbrush

1 Draw fish and starfish outlines on a sheet of paper. Turn the paper over and place it face-down on some newspaper.

2 Dip a toothbrush in yellow paint, then drag your finger over the bristles to spatter the paper. Try flicking yellow and orange paint with ordinary brushes, too.

3 Now flick blue and green paint on a second sheet of paper. Use different shades of blue and green to make a speckly sea background.

Top tip
Paint spattering is messy! Wear an overall, and spread out plenty of newspaper to work on.

Follow the steps above to create this speckly underwater scene

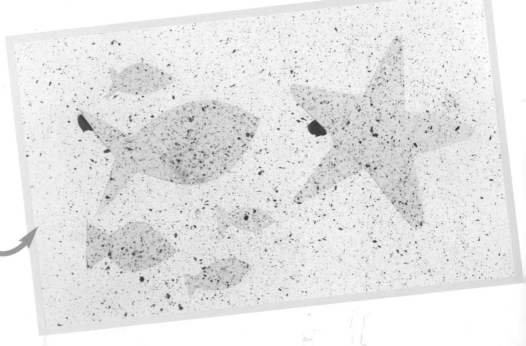

Click for Art!

To see 'drip paintings' by the American artist Jackson Pollock, go to **http://www.artlex.com/** and search for 'Action painting'.

4 When the paint is dry, turn the paper over and cut out the fish and starfish with safety scissors. Arrange them on your sea background and glue them down.

Desert landscape

1 Make card **stencils** using the shapes below.

2 Arrange the stencils on a sheet of thick cartridge paper. Use a small dab of glue to hold them in place.

3 Spatter yellow paint over the bottom part of the paper for the sand. Spatter blue paint above for the sky.

Copy these shapes onto card to create the desert landscape above

4 When the paint is dry, remove the card stencils.

Straw paintings

Blowing paint through a straw makes the paint wander in wiggly lines and creates wonderful and unusual shapes.

You will need:
A plastic drinking straw

1 Add water to some poster or acrylic paint to make the paint runny.

2 Drip a large blob of paint onto your paper with a brush.

Top tip
To mix colours, add a second colour when the first is still wet. If you do not want your colours to mix, wait until the first colour is dry before you add another.

12

3 Gently blow the paint through the straw. The paint will spread across the paper in wiggly lines.

4 Add different colours one by one. (See Top tip for hints on colour mixing.)

5 Add details with a crayon or brush to complete your painting.

Sometimes a straw painting may start to look like something recognizable – such as a fluffy chick, a flower, a person's hair or an insect.

This straw painting was made into a tree by adding a trunk with a brush

This chick's legs, eyes and beak were added with pencil and orange crayon

Click for Art! To explore paintings by Jackson Pollock, Mark Rothko and Robert Rauschenberg, go to **www.sfmoma.org/anderson/** Click on 'Start project' and then on 'Explore 15 works'.

Mirror paintings

By folding a painted piece of paper, you can make pictures that are **symmetrical** (the same on both sides).

You will need:
- A large sheet of cartridge paper
- Soft pencil for sketching

1 Make a crease in your sheet of paper by folding it in half lengthways then opening it out again. Paint a band of green across the middle, just above the crease.

2 Paint in a pale blue sky. Dab the paint with cotton wool to make white patches that look like clouds.

3 While the paint is still wet, fold the paper in half and press it down.

Top tip
Try other mirror art scenes, such as the sun setting over the sea.

4 Leave the paper folded for a minute then carefully open it out.

Click for Art!

To see an online gallery of children's art, go to **www.english.barnekunst.no/default.htm**

Brilliant butterfly

1 Fold a piece of cartridge paper in half. On one side, paint half the body and the wings of a butterfly. Use thick paints and work quickly.

2 While the paint is still wet, fold the paper down the middle and press the white side onto the painted side.

3 Leave for a minute, then carefully peel open the paper.

5 Working quickly, paint a row of trees. Paint the trunks brown and dab on blobs of orange, red and yellow for the leaves.

6 Fold the paper as before, then open it out. You should see a paler row of trees at the bottom of the page, looking like a reflection in a river.

Dotty paintings

To blend colours, try using a pattern of different-coloured dots and dashes.

You will need:
A paintbrush with a fine tip

Mixing colours

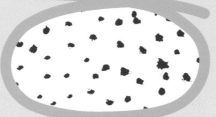

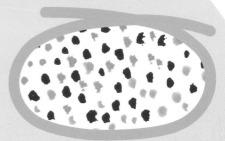

1 Before you begin your picture, practise making lots of tiny dots next to each other with the tip of your brush. Try one colour first, such as red.

2 Now make some more red dots on a clean sheet of paper. This time, space out the dots a bit.

3 When the red paint has dried, add yellow dots in between. Stand back. What colour do the red and yellow dots look like from a distance?

4 Now try making dots and dashes with different colours and different-sized brushes.

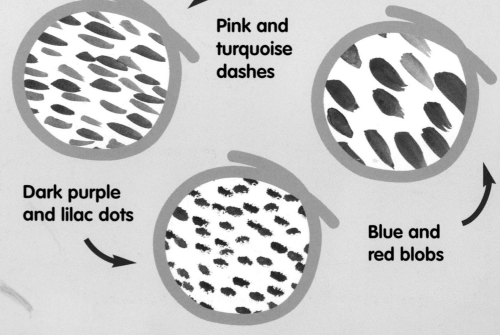

Pink and turquoise dashes

Dark purple and lilac dots

Blue and red blobs

16

Frog on a lily pad

Yellow dots highlight the frog's back

Top tip
Make darker dots and place them closer together to add detail and shading.

1 Plan your painting in your sketchbook or on a piece of scrap paper.

2 Lightly sketch the outline of your painting on a sheet of cartridge paper.

3 Colour each part of the picture with tiny dots of colour. This dotty painting has dark green for the lily pads, pale green for the frog, and yellow and dark green dots for the frog's markings.

Click for Art!
To learn how the French painter Seurat made paintings out of tiny dots, go to **www.metmuseum.org/Works_of_Art/** and search for 'Circus Sideshow'.

17

Wax paintings

Use paint and wax crayons to make wax **resist** paintings. The wax resists the paint so the colour of the crayons shows through.

1 Cover the bottom of your paper with white wax crayon for snow.

You will need:
- Thick paper or card
- Wax crayons
- Blue watercolour or poster paint

2 Still using wax crayons, add a snowman in the middle. Give him an orange carrot nose, two eyes, a black hat, some buttons and a stripy scarf.

3 Add lots of wax dots for falling snow.

4 Mix dark blue paint for the background. If you are using poster paint, add water to make it thinner.

Scraper effects

1 With wax crayon, create patches of bright colour on thick cartridge paper.

Top tip

If you are making a scraper picture, be sure to use thick paper or card, as ordinary paper may tear.

2 Paint three layers of black, dark blue or purple acrylic paint over the crayon.

3 When the paint is dry, scrape a picture into the paint with a knitting needle. The bright colours will show through.

5 Brush the blue paint over your drawing. The wax crayon will resist the paint so your drawing stands out.

Lost in space!

To make this picture, draw the rocket, planets and stars first using bright wax crayons. Then add black water-colour paint on top.

Water paintings

Enjoy experimenting with watercolour paints. They are great for seas and skies!

You will need:
- Watercolour paper
- Watercolour paints
- A wide brush
- A thin, pointed brush
- A sponge, tissue paper or cotton wool

3 Paint the sea using shorter brushstrokes. Use orange, yellow and blue. Let the colours run a little.

1 With a brush, paint clean water all over your sheet of watercolour paper.

2 Paint yellow stripes over the top half of your paper. Add orange stripes halfway down.

Top tip
To help the colours in the sea run together, drip a few drops of clean water over the paint.

4 While the paint is still wet, dab cotton wool on the yellow sky so the patches look like pale clouds.

5 When the paint is dry, paint a black island and a palm tree. If you like, add a shark's fin pointing out of the water!

Watery skies

For cloudy skies, paint overlapping stripes of blue watercolour paint across your paper. Before the paint dries, dab it with a clean sponge. This will leave white patches that look like clouds.

These clouds were made by painting stripes of blue across wet paper, then dabbing the paint with scrunched-up tissue paper

For a different effect, let the blue paint dry, then paint clouds in white watercolour paint

Click for Art!

To see watercolours by the English artist Turner, go to **www.j-m-w-turner.co.uk/** Click on 'Turner in Venice', scroll down, then click on small pictures.

Special effects

Make your paintings special by adding glitter or cornflour to paint, or sprinkling salt onto wet paint.

You will need:
- Glitter
- Cornflour
- Soft, wide brush
- Salt crystals

1 Wet the paper all over with a soft, wide brush.

2 While the paper is wet, drip blobs of paint in a circle and let them spread.

3 Add a tiny dot of paint for the centre of each flower. Sprinkle grains of salt over the painted petals. Watch how the salt soaks up the paint and makes dappled marks on the paper.

Flower painting

When the paint is dry, add stems for the flowers with a thin brush

Top tip

Shake off the salt when the paint has dried, or leave it on if you want more texture in your painting.

Click for Art!

For a good general children's art website including art galleries, art quizzes and information about artists and their work, visit **www.scribbleskidsart.com**

All that glitters

It's easy to make your own sparkly glitter paint. Just add glitter to acrylic or poster paint and paint it on with a brush as usual.

Adding texture

To thicken poster paint, add a few spoonfuls of cornflour. Keep mixing until you have the texture you want. Paint with a brush as usual. If you like, make patterns in the paint with a tool or card comb (see page 9).

23

Glossary

acrylic easy-to-mix paint that dries quickly and can be cleaned with soap and water

bristles fibres on the end of a paintbrush made of animal hair or nylon

cartridge paper thick, smooth paper, good for drawing and painting

palette a flat piece of wood or plastic used by artists to mix paints

PVA strong white glue that can be mixed with water; good for sticking paper and card

resist substance such as wax that protects a surface so it does not get coloured with paint or dye

sketchbook a small, easy-to-carry book for quick drawings and designs

stencil a shape cut-out of card which you can paint or print through, or around

symmetrical a shape that is the same on both sides

texture the surface or 'feel' of something – for example, fabric can be rough, soft, furry or velvety

watercolour paint paint sold in tubes or as small solid blocks

Index